contents

asian hot & spicy

introduction

Over the past few years in Western countries, there has been an incredible increase in interest in Asian cuisine. The traditions and secrets of Asian communities have spread across the world and established an ongoing love affair with Asian food and flavors.

With its fresh ingredients and minimal cooking times, Asian cuisine has come to symbolize simplicity, earthy goodness and exotic flavors. And Westerners have come to understand that it is the combination of flavors and cooking styles that we can create which makes our experiences with Asian cuisine so notable.

Nothing embodies the mysteries of Asia like the herbs and spices used. They are as versatile as they are special and they are as varied as there are dialects.

While it is virtually impossible to note every herb and spice used across Asia, this book has set out to introduce the beginner to a range of luscious, life-changing experiences, using Asian herbs and spices, and to give the experienced cook a great variety of new ideas.

Using gorgeous photography, this book offers an inspiring introduction to the incredible variety of chili peppers, Asian herbs and spices, while demonstrating the enormous range of dishes that can be prepared utilizing these ingredients.

There are traditional dishes such as chili-noodle cakes, red curry noodles with green vegetables, steamed seafood dumplings and stir-fried choy sum with ginger. But there are also dishes that blend the flavors of Asia with many other cultures, from the West to the Mediterranean. Combinations such as star anise and roast duck risotto, rustic potato soup with Thai spices, vichyssoise with Thai herbs, and chili beef burgers with Asian salad are wonderful examples of the contemporary creations that can be achieved using a little imagination and some knowledge of Asian herbs and spices.

For lovers of Asian drinks and desserts, you will be impressed with the mango and cumin lassi, pistachio and cardamom ice cream and the ginger and nutmeg sweet potato pudding.

The chilies, herbs and spices used in this book can be added, subtracted or substituted to suit individual tastes. Whether you are a lover of hot, fiery flavors or of subtle, tangy aromas, you will find a suitable recipe in this book.

The Asian cuisine is like no other. *Asian Hot & Spicy* will help you to explore this tantalizing world of flavor.

chili peppers

The chili peppers most commonly used in Asian cooking are small, red, hot chilies, and the longer, milder red and green chilies. Generally, the rule of thumb is the smaller the chili, the more fiery it tastes. Color, however, is not a reliable indication of a chili's pungency, with small green chilies sometimes more pungent than red ones.

Fresh chili peppers should be firm, glossy and evenly colored. Avoid chilies that are musty, soft or bruised. The best way to store fresh chili peppers is to wrap them well in paper towels, then place them in a plastic bag. They can be stored in the refrigerator for up to a week. Purchase dried chilies in small amounts and keep them in a cool dry place. Use them as soon as possible for optimum flavor.

Many people find chili peppers an intimidating food both to handle and to consume. The volatile oils in a fresh chili can burn the skin on contact (see page 11 for step-by-step preparation). Therefore it is wise to wear disposable plastic gloves when handling chilies and always wash your hands well with soap afterward. If you eat a chili dish that is too hot, consuming bread, rice, yogurt or milk will help tame the heat. Do not drink beer or sparkling drinks.

The recipes in this book call for chilies in amounts that may seem daunting. If you are unaccustomed to cooking with chili peppers, you may want to use fewer chilies than called for in a recipe and gradually raise your tolerance level. The heat or bite of a chili can be reduced by removing its seeds and white membrane. You can also achieve a milder flavor by adding chilies to a dish during cooking, then lifting them out and discarding them before serving. Remember, it's good etiquette to warn your guests that a dish you're serving contains chilies. But if you want the authentic fiery quality of various Asian cuisines, prepare the recipes as directed, using the full amount of fresh chilies.

Seeds are the hottest part. For making sambals, the chilies are used seeds and all, generally ground or puréed in a blender (such as the Indonesian sambal oelek).

If frying dried chilies as an accompaniment to a meal, use them whole, dropping them straight into hot oil. If they are being soaked and ground for a sauce or curry, first break or snip off the stalk end and shake to loosen and discard the seeds. Though dried chilies contribute plenty of heat and flavor to a dish, they do not have as severe an effect on the skin as fresh chilies.

Dried chilies are safe enough to handle until they have been soaked and ground, after which you should remember to wash your hands at once.

Bird's eye (left)
Used in Thai cooking, bird's eye chilies are blazing hot, with a clear, fiery taste. These small green or red chilies, about $\frac{1}{2}$ inch (12 mm) long, should be used in small quantities. Heat rating: ***

Serrano (right)
This widely available, green or red chili has thick flesh and a strong, pronounced heat. Slim and tapered, it reaches 2 inches (5 cm) long. Heat rating: ***

Jalapeño (left)
Popular and widely available, this Mexican chili, about 2 inches (5 cm) long, has thick flesh and delivers moderate heat. Green and ripe red chilies are sold in most markets. Heat rating: **

Habanero (right)
Considerable heat is packed into this small chili pepper, one of the hottest used in cooking. The habanero, measuring about 2 inches (5 cm) long and about as wide, varies from green to orange or red when ripe. Heat rating: ***

Thai green (left)
This medium-hot chili pepper, also known as Thai dragon, grows up to $1\frac{1}{2}$ inches (4 cm) long. The somewhat milder, green Anaheim chili pepper, similarly shaped and up to 6 inches (15 cm) long, may be substituted. Heat rating: **

Thai red (right)
The ripe counterpart to the Thai green chili pepper is also medium-hot and up to $1\frac{1}{2}$ inches (4 cm) long. The red Anaheim chili pepper or the red Dutch chili pepper may be used in its place. Heat rating: **

Dried Red Chilies   Chili Powder   Chili Oil   Sambal Oelek   Chili Pepper Flakes

Preparation of a fresh chili

Take special care not to touch your face or eyes when handling chilies, and always wash your hands thoroughly with soap and hot water afterwards. Alternatively, wear disposable gloves.

1 Using a sharp knife, trim the stem from the chili.

2 Cut the chili in half lengthwise.

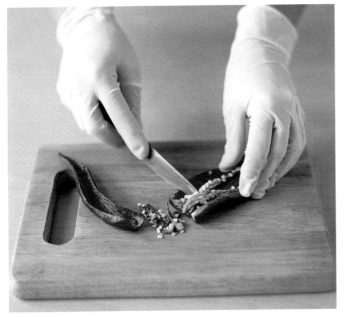

3 Scrape the seeds and the white pith (membrane) from the skin. The seeds contain some heat, but the real source of heat is the capsaicin, found in the white pith. Some recipes leave in the seeds for a hotter flavor.

4 Slice or chop the chili as required.

herbs and spices

Asian cooks make superb use of an extensive array of fresh and dried herbs and spices, and other seasonings. From fresh cilantro (fresh coriander), galangal and ginger to saffron, cardamom, and cumin seeds, these seasonings are combined to give Asian dishes their characteristic complexity and appealing richness.

The main flavorings used are ginger, garlic, and cilantro (coriander), and these are the flavorings with which Westerners have become most familiar, and have adapted across a wide range of dishes and styles. The less well-known spices, such as galangal and cardamom, will become familiar to you as you learn how to prepare creative, delicious meals.

The secret to Asian cooking is not so much matching herb to vegetable or meat, but learning to combine herbs and spices in order to achieve a range of subtle, strong, tangy, and always interesting flavors.

Basil, garlic, and chili are a popular combination for Thai cooking. The Vietnamese love garlic and coriander. The Chinese prefer a subtle blending of sweet and sour, hence the use of lemongrass, ginger, and star anise.

This book will show you how to make the best of the pale stalks of lemongrass, which add an intense lemon flavor; how to use the fragrant leaves from the kaffir lime tree, with their enticing citrus flavor; and how to use Vietnamese mint to create a spicy hot flavor to add to your salads and vegetables.

Purchase fresh herbs and spices for immediate use. Store them in a plastic bag in the refrigerator. When buying small dried spices, it's better to buy in small quantities and store in a cool, dark place and use as soon as possible for best results.

If you are an expert and wish to grow and dry your own herbs, here are a few hints. Correctly dried herbs always taste stronger than the fresh, as only the watery content has evaporated, leaving a concentration of essential oils. Whole dried leaves, or chopped or crumbled dried leaves are more powerful in fragrance and taste than powdered herbs, which often include ground stalks as well.

The opportunities to create new flavors using Asian herbs and spices are endless. Most importantly, each combination can be adapted to suit personal tastes. Let *Asian Hot & Spicy* open up a whole new world of flavor.

basil
Sweet-tasting herb whose leaves have slight licorice undertones.

betel leaves
These edible leaves are thick, smooth and dark in color. They are used mainly to wrap foods and they vary in size, from as big as a palm or bigger.

cilantro
Pungent, fragrant leaves from the coriander plant, resembling parsley and also called Chinese parsley and fresh coriander. The leaves, stems, and roots are all essential seasonings in Asian cooking.

galangal
A rhizome with a sharp flavor, sometimes called Thai ginger. Fresh galangal should be peeled before use, then sliced or grated. Galangal is also available dried.

garlic chive
This variety of chive, a relative of onions and leeks, has a strong garlic flavor. The flowers are also edible.

ginger
Thick rootlike rhizome of the ginger plant, with a sharp, pungent flavor. Once the tan skin is peeled from fresh ginger, the flesh is grated or sliced.

kaffir lime leaves
Fragrant leaves from the kaffir lime tree used fresh or dried, whole or shredded, for their enticing citrus flavor.

lemongrass
Pale stalks of a tropical grass that contribute an intense lemon flavor to Southeast Asian dishes. After the green blades are removed, the stalks are bruised or sliced before use.

mint
This aromatic herb is used extensively in Asian cooking. Fresh mint is preferred over dried.

Thai basil
Also known as holy basil, this variety of the popular herb has a strong, distinctive flavor.

Vietnamese mint
Spicy hot, this variety of mint makes a delicious addition to Asian salads.

cumin seeds

whole nutmeg

saffron threads

(left) The green or white (bleached) husk and consequently the whole pod has very little odor until it has been crushed. The seed has a pleasant aromatic odor and a warm, slightly pungent, highly aromatic taste.

star anise

cardamom pods

asian cooking

The size and shape of the wok make it ideal for stir-frying and for steaming and deep-frying Asian-style foods. Carbon steel or rolled steel woks, the popular inexpensive types found in Asian markets, are coated with a thin film of lacquer to prevent rusting. This film needs to be removed before the wok can be used. The best way to do this is to place the wok on the stove top, fill with cold water and add 2 tablespoons baking soda (bicarbonate of soda). Bring to a boil and boil rapidly for 15 minutes. Drain and scrub off the coating with a plastic scouring pad. Repeat the process if any lacquer remains. Then rinse and dry the wok. It is now ready to be seasoned.

Carbon steel, rolled steel and cast iron woks require seasoning, which prevents discoloration and creates a smooth surface that will help keep food from sticking. To season a wok, place it over low heat. Have handy vegetable oil and paper towels. When the wok is hot, carefully wipe it with an oiled paper towel. Repeat the process with fresh towels until the towels come away clean, without any trace of color.

A seasoned wok should not be scrubbed clean with detergent. Instead, use hot water and a sponge. Dry the wok well after washing. Store in a dry, well-ventilated place. Long periods without use can cause the oil coating on the wok to become rancid. If oil on a wok becomes rancid, then season once again and it's ready to use. Using your wok is the best way to prevent this from occurring.

A number of cooking utensils are used with a wok. Bamboo steamers, with lids, are available in many sizes to fit inside a variety of woks. Steamers can be stacked on top of each other over simmering water in a wok, allowing many items to be cooked at once. Bamboo steamers need only be rinsed in hot water after use.

A slotted spoon for removing deep-fried foods from hot oil, a good-quality cleaver for chopping ingredients and long chopsticks for handling cooked foods – as well as a lid for your wok – are other handy items to acquire for cooking Asian recipes.

Spicy squash and bean soup

2 tablespoons olive oil

3 scallions (shallots / spring onions), finely sliced

12 oz (375 g) carrots, peeled and sliced

5 oz (150 g) rutabaga (swede), peeled and cubed

2 celery stalks, sliced

1 lb (500 g) butternut squash (pumpkin), peeled and cubed

1 small red chili pepper, seeded and sliced

$^3/_4$ cup (5 oz / 150 g) drained, canned cannellini beans

6 cups (48 fl oz / 1.5 L) vegetable stock or water

1 bay leaf

6 sprigs of fresh cilantro (fresh coriander), leaves removed and stems tied with kitchen string

1 cup (8 fl oz / 250 ml) cream

2 tablespoons chopped fresh Vietnamese mint, for garnish

2 tablespoons chopped fresh cilantro (fresh coriander), for garnish

Warm olive oil in large pan over medium heat. Add scallions, carrots, rutabaga, celery, squash and chili pepper and cook until vegetables soften slightly, about 6 minutes. Add beans, stock, bay leaf and cilantro leaves and stems. Bring to a boil. Cover, reduce heat to low and cook until vegetables are tender, about 15 minutes. Remove cilantro stems and discard.

Working in batches, purée soup in a food processor or blender. Return to saucepan and heat through, about 3 minutes. Ladle into bowls and swirl ¼ cup (2 fl oz / 60 ml) cream into each serving. Combine chopped mint and cilantro. Garnish soup with herbs and serve immediately.

Serves 4

Hint

Bird's eye and serrano chilies are recommended for this recipe.

Rustic potato soup with Thai spices

Warm olive oil in a large saucepan over medium heat. Add onion and garlic and cook until onion softens, about 2 minutes. Add potatoes, cilantro, parsley, 4 lime leaves, ginger and chili pepper and cook for 1 minute. Add stock and bring to a boil. Reduce heat to simmer, cover and cook until potatoes are tender, 20–25 minutes. Remove lime leaves and discard.

Break up some of the potatoes with a potato masher, keeping texture of soup chunky. Season with salt and pepper. Add coconut milk and heat through, about 2 minutes. Serve warm, garnishing each portion with a lime leaf.

Serves 4

2 tablespoons olive oil

1 yellow (brown) onion, chopped

2 cloves garlic, chopped

20 oz (625 g) potatoes,
   peeled and roughly chopped

2 tablespoons chopped fresh cilantro
   (fresh coriander)

2 tablespoons chopped fresh Continental parsley

4 fresh kaffir lime leaves
   or 1 teaspoon grated lime zest

1 tablespoon peeled and grated fresh ginger

1 small red chili pepper, seeded and chopped

6 cups (48 fl oz / 1.5 L) vegetable stock or water

salt and pepper

1½ cups (12 fl oz / 375 ml) coconut milk

4 fresh kaffir lime leaves
   or 1 teaspoon grated lime zest, for garnish

Hint

Bird's eye and serrano chilies are recommended for this recipe.

Asian vegetable and lentil soup

3 tablespoons peanut oil

2 tablespoons peeled and grated fresh ginger

1 small red chili pepper,
   seeded and finely sliced

$1/_4$ teaspoon ground cumin

$1/_4$ teaspoon curry powder

1 small red (Spanish) onion, chopped

1 small parsnip, peeled and sliced

2 celery stalks, thinly sliced

4 large carrots, peeled and sliced

1 potato, peeled and sliced

2 kaffir lime leaves
   or $1/_2$ teaspoon grated lime zest

$1/_2$ cup (3 $1/_2$ oz / 105 g) red or brown lentils

6 cups (48 fl oz / 1.5 L) vegetable stock or water

1 cup (8 fl oz / 250 ml) coconut milk

2 tablespoons chopped fresh cilantro
   (fresh coriander), for garnish

Warm peanut oil in a large saucepan over medium heat. Add ginger, chili pepper, cumin and curry powder and cook until aromatic, about 1 minute. Add onion, parsnip, celery, carrots, potato and lime leaves. Cover and cook, stirring occasionally, for 10 minutes. Add lentils and stock and bring to a boil. Cover and cook until vegetables and lentils are soft, about 20 minutes. Remove lime leaves and discard.

Working in batches, purée soup in a food processor. Return to saucepan, add coconut milk and heat through, about 3 minutes. Garnish with chopped cilantro and serve.

Serves 4

Hint

Bird's eye and serrano chilies are recommended for this recipe.

Vichyssoise with Thai herbs

Trim root and green section from leek and discard. Slice white portion and rinse under cold running water to remove all dirt. Melt butter in a large saucepan over medium heat. Add leek and cook until softened, about 5 minutes. Add potatoes and stock, cover and cook until potatoes are tender, about 30 minutes.

To make Thai herbs:

Combine all ingredients and mix well. Set aside until serving.

Working in batches, purée soup in a food processor. Return to saucepan and heat through, 3–5 minutes. Season with salt and pepper. Ladle soup into bowls and swirl 2 tablespoons coconut milk into each serving. Garnish with a spoonful of Thai herbs.

Serves 6

4 leeks

1/4 cup (2 oz / 60 g) butter

1 1/2 lb (750 g) potatoes, peeled and cubed

8 cups (64 fl oz / 2 L) vegetable stock or water

sea salt and freshly ground black pepper

1 cup (8 fl oz / 250 ml) coconut milk

FOR THAI HERBS

2 cloves garlic, chopped

1/4 cup (1/4 oz / 7 g) loosely packed fresh
    Continental parsley leaves

1/4 cup chopped fresh cilantro (fresh coriander)

1/4 small red chili pepper, seeded and chopped

grated zest (rind) of 1/2 lemon

Hint

Bird's eye and serrano chilies are recommended for this recipe.

Bok choy and potato soup

¹/₄ cup (2 oz / 60 g) butter

2 red (Spanish) onions, chopped

1 clove garlic, chopped

1 piece fresh ginger, about 1 inch (2.5 cm) long,
   peeled and chopped

6 cups (48 fl oz / 1.5 L) chicken
   or vegetable stock

20 oz (625 g) potatoes, peeled and chopped

8 oz (250 g) bok choy, tough stems discarded,
   leaves sliced

1 bunch spinach, stems discarded, leaves sliced

salt and pepper

2 tablespoons soy sauce

14 oz (440 g) udon noodles

1 cup (4 oz / 125 g) snow pea (mange-tout)
   sprouts, for garnish

Melt butter in a large saucepan over medium heat. Add onions, garlic and ginger and cook until onions and garlic are soft, about 2 minutes. Add stock and bring to a boil. Add potatoes, reduce heat to simmer, cover and cook until tender, about 10 minutes.

Add bok choy and spinach. Season with salt and pepper. Stir in soy sauce and noodles. Cook until noodles are done, about 5 minutes. Ladle into bowls and garnish with snow pea sprouts.

Serves 4

Carrot soup with Asian greens and coconut

Place carrots, onion, garlic and stock in a large saucepan. Bring to a boil. Cover and cook until carrots are soft, about 8 minutes. Working in batches, purée soup in a food processor. Return to saucepan and reheat over medium heat, about 5 minutes.

Add greens, lime juice and basil and cook for 2 minutes. Ladle into bowls and top each serving with 1 tablespoon coconut cream. Sprinkle with shredded coconut.

Serves 4

2 lb (1 kg) carrots, peeled and finely diced

1 large yellow (brown) onion, chopped

2 cloves garlic, chopped

6 cups (48 fl oz / 1.5 L) chicken or vegetable stock

6½ oz (200 g) Asian greens such as bok choy or choy sum, roughly sliced

juice of 1 lime

1 tablespoon chopped Thai basil leaves

4 tablespoons thick coconut cream, for serving

¼ cup (1 oz / 30 g) unsweetened dried (desiccated) shredded coconut, toasted, for garnish

noodles

Star anise and roast duck risotto

½ Chinese roast duck

6 cups (48 fl oz / 1.5 L) chicken stock

3 star anise

1 piece fresh ginger, about 2 inches (5 cm) long

4 tablespoons olive oil

6 scallions (shallots / spring onions),
  white and pale green parts, finely sliced

5 oz (150 g) fresh shiitake mushrooms, sliced

1 small red bell pepper (capsicum),
  seeded and chopped

1⅓ cups (9 oz / 280 g) arborio rice

Remove meat and skin from duck and discard bones. Cut meat and skin into bite-sized pieces, about 1½ inches (4 cm). Cover and refrigerate until ready to use. Place stock, star anise and ginger in a saucepan and bring to a boil. Reduce heat to simmer, cover and cook for 20 minutes. Strain stock into another saucepan and discard star anise and ginger. Bring stock to a simmer over low heat.

In a saucepan over medium heat, warm 2 tablespoons olive oil. Add scallions, mushrooms and bell pepper and cook until mushrooms soften, 2–3 minutes. Transfer mushroom mixture to a bowl and set aside.

In a saucepan over medium heat, warm remaining 2 tablespoons olive oil. Add rice and cook, stirring constantly, until rice grains are evenly coated with oil, about 2 minutes. Add 1 cup (8 fl oz / 250 ml) hot stock to rice, reduce heat to simmer and cook, stirring constantly, until liquid is absorbed. Add remaining stock, 1 cup (8 fl oz / 250 ml) at a time, continuing to stir constantly, until rice is al dente and creamy. Add duck and mushroom mixture and stir gently until heated through. Serve immediately.

Serves 4–6

Saffron rice parcels

Place rice in a bowl and add cold water to cover. Cover and allow to stand for 4 hours. Drain and rinse. Place rice in a heatproof bowl. Add brown sugar, saffron, coconut milk, water and zest. Mix until well combined. Place bowl in a large bamboo steamer.

Half fill a large wok with water (steamer should not touch water) and bring to a boil. Place steamer in wok, cover and cook rice, stirring often and adding more water to wok when necessary, until all liquid has been absorbed and rice is tender, about 45 minutes. Lift steamer from wok, carefully remove bowl of rice from steamer and allow to cool.

Lay a banana leaf on a work surface and spoon 1 tablespoon rice into middle. Top with a banana slice. Fold leaf over rice to form a parcel. Secure with kitchen string.

Arrange parcels in steamer. Place steamer in wok over boiling water, cover and cook parcels for 10 minutes. Lift steamer from wok and remove parcels from steamer. Serve warm as part of an Asian banquet or at the end of a spicy meal.

Makes 15 parcels

1 cup (6¹/₂ oz / 200 g) white glutinous rice
2 tablespoons brown sugar
1 teaspoon saffron threads
²/₃ cup (5 fl oz / 150 ml) coconut milk
³/₄ cup (6 fl oz / 180 ml) water
grated zest (rind) of 1 lime
8–10 young banana leaves,
   rinsed and cut into 7-inch (18-cm) squares,
   or 15 squares of aluminum foil
2 bananas, peeled and sliced
juice of 1 lime

Chili-noodle cakes

6¹/₂ oz (200 g) fresh thin egg noodles

3¹/₂ cups (3¹/₂ oz / 105 g) spinach leaves,
  stems removed

1 small red chili pepper,
  seeded and finely chopped

¹/₂ red bell pepper (capsicum),
  seeded and chopped

6¹/₂ oz (200 g) fresh or canned crabmeat,
  well drained

juice and grated zest (rind) of 1 lime

¹/₄ cup (¹/₃ oz / 10 g) chopped fresh Thai basil

1 egg, beaten

¹/₂ cup (2 oz / 60 g) cornstarch (cornflour)

¹/₃ cup (3 fl oz / 90 ml) vegetable oil, for frying

¹/₂ cup (4 fl oz / 125 ml) Thai sweet chili sauce,
  for dipping

Preheat oven to 225°F (110°C / Gas ¼). Fill a saucepan with water and bring to a boil. Add noodles and cook until tender, about 3 minutes. (Some precooked fresh egg noodles need only to be soaked in hot water for 8 minutes; check package for instructions.) Drain noodles and set aside.

Bring a saucepan half filled with water to a boil. Remove from heat and plunge spinach leaves into water. Immediately drain and rinse under cold running water. Squeeze out any excess liquid from spinach. Chop spinach finely.

In a large bowl, combine noodles, spinach, chili pepper, bell pepper, crabmeat, lime zest and juice, basil, egg and cornstarch. Using wet hands, mix until well combined. Shape noodle mixture into patties using 2 tablespoons per patty.

Warm vegetable oil in a deep frying pan or saucepan over medium heat. Working in batches, cook patties in hot oil, turning once, until golden, about 1½ minutes per side. Using a slotted spoon, remove from pan and drain on paper towels. Place in an ovenproof pan lined with parchment (baking) paper and keep warm in preheated oven. Serve warm with chili sauce for dipping.

Serves 6–8

Hint

Bird's eye and serrano chilies are recommended for this recipe.

Red curry noodles with green vegetables

Bring a saucepan of water to a boil. Add noodles and cook until tender, about 3 minutes. (Some precooked noodles need only to be soaked in hot water for 8 minutes; check package for instructions.) Drain noodles and set aside.

In a saucepan over low heat, combine coconut milk, red curry paste, tamarind pulp, fish sauce and sugar. Stir until heated through, about 5 minutes; do not boil. Add beans and choy sum and simmer until vegetables soften slightly, about 3 minutes. Add noodles and bean sprouts and stir until heated through, about 2 minutes. Serve hot, sprinkled with peanuts.

Serves 4

8 oz (250 g) fresh egg noodles

1½ cups (12 fl oz / 375 ml) coconut milk

2½ tablespoons red curry paste
(see page 54 for recipe)

2 tablespoons tamarind pulp

3 teaspoons fish sauce

1 teaspoon superfine (caster) sugar

5 oz (150 g) long beans, trimmed and cut into
2½-inch (6-cm) lengths

1 bunch (16 oz / 500 g) choy sum, trimmed
and leaves cut into 2½-inch (6-cm) lengths

2 cups (8 oz / 250 g) bean sprouts

⅓ cup (2 oz / 60 g) unsalted roasted peanuts

Fish wraps

1 lb (500 g) firm white-fleshed fish fillets

2 teaspoons peeled and grated fresh ginger

2 tablespoons Thai sweet chili sauce

6 scallions (shallots / spring onions), chopped

1 tablespoon fish sauce

1 egg, beaten

1/2 cup (1 oz / 30 g) fresh white breadcrumbs

2 tablespoons chopped fresh cilantro
  (fresh coriander)

32 betel leaves

32 toothpicks

1/2 cup (4 fl oz / 125 ml) Thai sweet chili sauce,
  for dipping

Place fish in a food processor and process until a thick paste is formed, about 30 seconds. Add ginger, chili sauce, scallions, fish sauce, egg, breadcrumbs and cilantro. Process until well combined, about 10 seconds. Using wet hands, divide mixture into 32 portions and shape into balls.

Line a medium-sized bamboo steamer with parchment (baking) paper. Half fill a medium-sized wok with water (steamer should not touch water) and bring water to a boil. Working in batches, arrange fish balls in steamer. Cover, place over boiling water and steam until cooked through, about 15 minutes, adding more water to wok when necessary. Lift steamer from wok and carefully remove fish balls. Wrap each ball in a betel leaf and skewer with a toothpick. Serve warm with chili sauce for dipping.

Makes 32

Hint

Use butter lettuce leaves or basil leaves if betel leaves are unavailable.

Steamed seafood dumplings

Place fish fillets and shrimp in a food processor and process until a thick paste forms, about 30 seconds. Add ginger, chili pepper, cilantro, scallions, sesame oil, rice wine, soy sauce, salt and sugar. Process until well combined, about 10 seconds. Transfer to a bowl and mix in water chestnuts.

Place wonton wrappers on a work surface and keep covered with a damp kitchen towel to prevent drying. Working with one wrapper at a time, lay it on work surface and place 3 teaspoons filling in middle. Gather edges around filling to form a basket. Gently squeeze center of dumpling so that filling is exposed at top. Gently tap bottom of dumpling on work surface to flatten. Set aside, covered with plastic wrap, and repeat with remaining wrappers and filling.

Line a medium-sized bamboo steamer with parchment (baking) paper.

Half fill a medium-sized wok with water (steamer should not touch water) and bring to a boil. Arrange filled wontons in steamer. Cover steamer, place over boiling water and cook for 12 minutes, adding more water to wok when necessary. Lift steamer from wok and carefully remove dumplings. Serve warm with soy sauce for dipping.

Makes 18

8 oz (250 g) firm white-fleshed fish fillets

8 oz (250 g) jumbo shrimp (green king prawns), peeled and deveined

3 teaspoons peeled and grated fresh ginger

½ small red chili pepper, seeded and chopped

3 tablespoons chopped fresh cilantro (fresh coriander)

4 scallions (shallots / spring onions), chopped

1 teaspoon Asian sesame oil

1 teaspoon rice wine

1 teaspoon soy sauce

½ teaspoon salt

1 teaspoon sugar

6 canned water chestnuts, drained and finely chopped

18 round wonton wrappers

⅓ cup (3 fl oz / 90 ml) soy sauce, for dipping

Hint

Bird's eye and serrano chilies are recommended for this recipe.

Steamed lemon-pepper fish

1 whole snapper, about 1 lb (500 g)

4 kaffir lime leaves or 1 teaspoon
  grated lime zest

2 teaspoons fish sauce

2 teaspoons oyster sauce

1 tablespoon fresh lime juice

1 teaspoon Asian sesame oil

2 teaspoons peeled and grated ginger

1 lemongrass stalk, trimmed and finely sliced

8 garlic chives, finely chopped

1/2 teaspoon ground or whole roasted
  Szechwan peppercorns

lime halves, for serving

Using a sharp knife, make 3 deep slits in each side of fish. Place lime leaves in fish cavity. In a small bowl, combine fish sauce, oyster sauce, lime juice, sesame oil and ginger and brush over fish. Place fish on a lightly oiled heatproof plate that will fit inside a bamboo steamer. Sprinkle with lemongrass, garlic chives and pepper.

Half fill a large wok with water (steamer should not touch water) and bring to a boil. Place fish in steamer. Cover, place steamer over boiling water and cook until fish is done, about 20 minutes, adding more water to wok when necessary. Lift steamer from wok and carefully remove fish from steamer. Serve warm, drizzled with cooking juices and accompanied with lime halves.

Serves 2

Shrimp and lemongrass sticks

Place shrimp in a food processor and process until a thick paste forms, about 20 seconds. Add garlic, ginger, scallions, cilantro, sambal oelek, fish sauce and 2 tablespoons cornstarch and process until well combined, about 10 seconds. Using wet hands, divide mixture into 12 portions. Mold each portion around end of a lemongrass piece. Lightly dust with cornstarch, shaking off any excess.

Heat oil in a large wok until it reaches 375°F (190°C) on a deep-frying thermometer or until a small bread cube dropped in oil sizzles and turns golden. Working in batches, add lemongrass sticks and cook until golden, 3–4 minutes. Using a slotted spoon, remove from hot oil and drain on paper towels. Serve hot with soy sauce or chili oil for dipping.

Makes 12

1½ lb (750 g) jumbo shrimp (green king prawns), peeled and deveined

3 cloves garlic, chopped

2 teaspoons peeled and grated fresh ginger

6 scallions (shallots / spring onions), chopped

¼ cup (⅓ oz / 10 g) chopped fresh cilantro (fresh coriander)

1 teaspoon sambal oelek (see page 52 for recipe)

3 teaspoons fish sauce

2 tablespoons cornstarch (cornflour)

6 lemongrass stalks, trimmed and cut into 12 pieces about 4 inches (10 cm) long

¼ cup (1 oz / 30 g) cornstarch (cornflour), for dusting

3 cups (24 fl oz / 750 ml) vegetable oil, for frying

soy sauce or chili oil (see page 52 for recipe), for dipping

Hint

Bird's eye and serrano chilies are recommended for this recipe.

Lime shrimp with spicy Thai pesto

FOR THAI PESTO

½ cup (2½ oz / 75 g) roasted unsalted peanuts

1 medium-sized green chili pepper,
   seeded and roughly chopped

1 cup (1 oz / 30 g) fresh Thai basil leaves

40 Vietnamese mint leaves

3 cloves garlic, peeled

1 teaspoon peeled and grated fresh ginger

juice of 1 lime

⅓ cup (3 fl oz / 90 ml) peanut oil

36 cooked jumbo shrimp (green king prawns),
   peeled and deveined, tails intact

12 small bamboo skewers

juice of 1 lime

1 clove garlic, peeled and chopped

To make pesto: Place peanuts, chili pepper, basil and mint leaves, garlic, ginger and lime juice in a food processor and process until finely ground, about 1 minute. With food processor running, add peanut oil in a steady stream. Blend until a thick paste forms. Spoon pesto into a screw-top jar and pour a little extra peanut oil over surface. Store in refrigerator until ready to use. (Pesto will keep for up to 2 weeks).

To serve, skewer 3 shrimp onto each bamboo skewer. Combine lime juice and garlic in a small bowl and brush over shrimp. Cover shrimp and place in the refrigerator for 30 minutes. Spoon pesto into small serving bowls. Place 3 skewers and a bowl of pesto on each plate.

Serves 4

Hint

Thai green (Thai dragon) and serrano chilies are recommended for this recipe.

Fried fish with chili sauce

To make chili sauce: Place chili peppers in a small bowl, add boiling water and soak for 30 minutes. Drain and finely chop. Warm oil in a small saucepan over medium heat. Add garlic and cook until aromatic, about 1 minute. Add chili sauce, ketchup, stock, sugar and chilies. Bring to a boil, reduce heat to simmer and cook for 3 minutes. Add cornstarch-water mixture and stir until sauce thickens slightly, about 3 minutes. Season with salt and set aside.

Remove root and green section of scallions. Cut into 2½-inch (6-cm) lengths. Slice each piece lengthwise into fine strips. Place in a bowl of ice water and refrigerate until scallions curl, about 15 minutes. Drain.

Preheat oven to 225°F (110°C / Gas ¼).

In a small bowl, whisk cornstarch and eggs together. Add fish pieces and stir gently until coated in batter. Heat oil in a wok or saucepan until it reaches 375°F (190°C) on a deep-frying thermometer or until a small bread cube dropped in oil sizzles and turns golden. Working in batches, lift fish, one piece at a time, from batter, allowing excess batter to drain off, and carefully place in hot oil. Cook until golden, turning once, 3–4 minutes total. Using a slotted spoon, remove fish from hot oil and drain on paper towels. Place on a heatproof dish and keep warm in preheated oven. Repeat with remaining fish. Place fish on individual plates, drizzle with chili sauce and top with scallion curls. Serve remaining chili sauce in a separate bowl.

Serves 6

FOR CHILI SAUCE
4 dried chili peppers
¼ cup (2 fl oz / 60 ml) boiling water
1 tablespoon vegetable oil
2 cloves garlic, finely chopped
2 tablespoons Chinese chili sauce
4 tablespoons tomato ketchup
1 cup (8 fl oz / 250 ml) chicken stock
1 teaspoon superfine (caster) sugar
2 teaspoons cornstarch (cornflour)
  mixed with 1 tablespoon water
sea salt to taste

3 scallions (shallots / spring onions)
1 tablespoon cornstarch (cornflour)
3 eggs, beaten
6 firm white-fleshed fish fillets,
  cut into 3-inch (7.5-cm) pieces
3 cups (24 fl oz / 750 ml) vegetable oil
  for deep-frying

Red curry shrimp

FOR STEAMED JASMINE RICE

2 cups jasmine rice

3 cups boiling water (from a kettle)

FOR SHRIMP

2 cups (16 fl oz / 500 ml) coconut milk

2 tablespoons red curry paste
  (see page 54 for recipe)

2 tablespoons fish sauce

1 long red chili pepper, halved and seeded

1½ lb (750 g) jumbo shrimp (green king prawns),
  peeled and deveined, tails intact

2 kaffir lime leaves, finely shredded or
  ½ teaspoon grated lime zest, for garnish

Place rice in a fine-mesh sieve and rinse with cold running water until water is clear. Drain and place in a saucepan with boiling water. Cover and bring to a boil over high heat. Reduce heat to low and cook for about 15 minutes. Remove from heat and stand for 5 minutes. Fluff with a fork.

In a saucepan over low heat, combine coconut milk, curry paste, fish sauce and chili pepper. Stir until heated through, about 5 minutes; do not boil. Add shrimp and cook, stirring, until shrimp change color, about 15 minutes. Serve hot with jasmine rice. Garnish with shredded lime leaves.

Serves 4

Hint

Thai red chilies are recommended for this recipe.

duck

Thai spicy chicken with basil

Warm vegetable and sesame oils in a wok or frying pan over medium heat. Add garlic, ginger and chili peppers and cook until aromatic, about 1 minute. Raise heat to high, add bell pepper and chicken and stir-fry until chicken is golden, about 5 minutes. Stir in soy sauce, water and brown sugar. Reduce heat to medium and cook until chicken is cooked through, about 5 minutes. Stir in basil and scallions. Spoon into bowls and serve with steamed jasmine rice.

Serves 4

2 tablespoons vegetable oil

2 teaspoons Asian sesame oil

3 cloves garlic, finely chopped

1 tablespoon peeled and grated fresh ginger

4 small red chili peppers, halved and seeded

1 red bell pepper (capsicum), seeded and sliced

1 lb (500 g) skinless chicken thigh fillets,
    cut into 1-inch (2.5-cm) cubes

2 tablespoons soy sauce

2 tablespoons water

2 teaspoons brown sugar

1/2 cup (1/2 oz / 15 g) fresh basil leaves

6 scallions (shallots / spring onions),
    cut diagonally into 1-inch (2.5-cm) lengths

steamed jasmine rice, for serving
    (see page 34 for recipe)

Duck on a bed of chili onions

4 tablespoons chili oil (see page 52 for recipe)

19 oz (590 g) yellow (brown) onions,
  thinly sliced

3 cloves garlic, finely chopped

1 small red chili pepper, seeded and sliced

4 duck or chicken breasts,
  4–5 oz (125–150 g) each

1 tablespoon ground ginger

1 tablespoon ground coriander

1 tablespoon ground black pepper

1 teaspoon sea salt

2 tablespoons vegetable oil, for frying

4 oz (125 g) sugar snap peas

1/4 cup (1/4 oz / 7 g) loosely packed small
  Thai basil leaves

Thai sweet chili sauce, for serving, optional

Preheat oven to 225°F (110°C / Gas 1/4). Warm 2 tablespoons chili oil in a frying pan over medium-low heat. Add onions, garlic and chili pepper and cook until onions are transparent and soft, about 10 minutes. Transfer to a heatproof dish and keep warm in preheated oven.

Using tip of a sharp knife, score skin side of each duck breast. In a small bowl, combine ginger, coriander, pepper and salt. Brush breasts with remaining 2 tablespoons chili oil. Rub breasts with spice mixture. Warm vegetable oil in a frying pan over medium heat. Add duck breasts and cook until golden and cooked through, 5–6 minutes per side. Remove from pan, place on a heatproof dish and keep warm in oven.

Bring a saucepan of water to a boil. Remove from heat, add sugar snap peas and cook for 1 minute. Immediately drain and rinse under cold running water. Drain.

Spoon onions onto plates. Cut each duck breast diagonally into 4–6 slices. Arrange slices over onions and garnish with basil. Serve with sugar snap peas and Thai sweet chili sauce.

Serves 4

Hint

Bird's eye and serrano chilies are recommended for this recipe.

Poached chicken in green coconut sauce

In a saucepan over low heat, combine coconut milk, curry paste, lime leaves, fish sauce and chili pepper. Stir until heated through, about 5 minutes; do not boil. Add chicken and cook, stirring, until tender, about 20 minutes. Serve hot with steamed jasmine rice. Garnish with cilantro leaves.

Serves 4

2½ cups (20 fl oz / 625 ml) coconut milk

2 tablespoons green curry paste
(see page 54 for recipe)

3 kaffir lime leaves
or 1 teaspoon grated lime zest

1 tablespoon fish sauce

1 long green chili pepper, halved

1 lb (500 g) skinless chicken thigh fillets,
cut into 1-inch (2.5-cm) cubes

steamed jasmine rice (see page 34 for recipe)

¼ cup (¼ oz / 7 g) fresh cilantro
(fresh coriander) leaves, for garnish

Hint

Thai green (Thai dragon) chili is recommended for this recipe.

Spicy oven-roasted chicken

1 chicken, about 3 lb (1.5 kg)

½ teaspoon saffron threads

1 tablespoon boiling water

6 cloves garlic, crushed

2 tablespoons peeled and grated fresh ginger

⅓ cup (3 fl oz / 90 ml) fresh lemon juice

½ teaspoon ground chili

2 teaspoons ground paprika

1 teaspoon salt

3 teaspoons garam masala

olive oil cooking spray

steamed jasmine rice (see page 34 for recipe)

Preheat oven to 350°F (180°C / Gas 4). Rinse and dry chicken. Truss chicken with kitchen string. In a small bowl, combine saffron and boiling water and soak for 10 minutes. Place saffron mixture in a food processor or blender. Add garlic, ginger, lemon juice, chili, paprika, salt and garam masala. Process until smooth. Rub spice mixture over chicken. Cover and refrigerate for 2–3 hours, or as long as over-night.

Spray chicken lightly with cooking oil spray. Place in an oiled roasting pan and cook until golden and tender and juices run clear when chicken is pierced with a sharp knife, about 1¼ hours. Serve hot or cold with steamed jasmine rice.

Serves 4

pork

Hot-and-spicy money bags

Place mushrooms in a small bowl, add boiling water to cover and let stand until softened, 10–15 minutes. Drain and squeeze excess liquid from mushrooms. Finely chop, discarding thick stems. In a bowl, combine mushrooms, shrimp, pork, chili peppers, cilantro, scallions, garlic, ginger, sesame oil, soy sauce and rice wine. Using wet hands, mix until well combined.

Place wonton wrappers on a work surface and keep covered with a damp kitchen towel to prevent drying. Working with one wonton wrapper at a time, lay it on work surface and place 1 teaspoon filling in middle. Brush edges with water. Gather edges and twist to seal. Repeat with remaining wrappers and filling.

Heat oil in a large wok until it reaches 375°F (190°C) on a deep-frying thermometer or until a small bread cube dropped in oil sizzles and turns golden. Working in batches, add wontons and fry until golden, 1–2 minutes. Using a slotted spoon, remove from hot oil and drain on paper towels. Serve hot with soy sauce for dipping.

Makes 20

6 Chinese dried mushrooms

4 oz (125 g) jumbo shrimp (green king prawns), peeled, deveined and finely chopped

12¹/₂ oz (375 g) ground (minced) pork

1 or 2 small red chili peppers, seeded, if desired, and finely chopped

¹/₃ cup (¹/₂ oz / 15 g) chopped fresh cilantro (fresh coriander)

6 scallions (shallots / spring onions), finely chopped

2 cloves garlic, finely chopped

3 teaspoons peeled and grated fresh ginger

2 teaspoons Asian sesame oil

3 teaspoons soy sauce

2 teaspoons rice wine

20 square wonton wrappers

4 cups (32 fl oz / 1 L) vegetable oil, for deep-frying

soy sauce, for dipping

Hint

Bird's eye and serrano chilies are recommended for this recipe.

Shredded pork on spicy bruschetta

1½ tablespoons Asian sesame oil

2 tablespoons chili oil (see page 52 for recipe)

¼ cup (2 fl oz / 60 ml) soy sauce

1 clove garlic, crushed

2 tablespoons rice wine vinegar or dry sherry

1 teaspoon peeled and grated fresh ginger

¼ cup (2 fl oz / 60 ml) olive oil

1 lb (500 g) yellow (brown) onions, sliced

¾ cup (6 fl oz / 180 ml) red wine vinegar

2 tablespoons sugar

2 tablespoons vegetable oil

13 oz (400 g) boneless pork fillets

4 thick slices wood-fired bread

3 oz (90 g) snow pea (mange-tout) sprouts

3 scallions (shallots / spring onions),
  trimmed and sliced diagonally

1 cup (1 oz / 30 g) loosely packed fresh cilantro
  (fresh coriander) leaves

To make dressing: Place sesame oil, chili oil, soy sauce, garlic, vinegar and ginger in a screwtop jar and shake to mix well. Set aside. Warm olive oil in a heavy-bottomed frying pan over medium heat. Add onions and cook until browned, about 5 minutes. Add vinegar, bring to a boil, reduce heat to low and add sugar. Cook, stirring occasionally, until onions caramelize, about 12 minutes.

Warm vegetable oil in a frying pan over medium heat. Add pork and cook until tender, 5–6 minutes per side. Remove from pan, cover with aluminum foil and allow to stand 10 minutes. Toast or grill bread slices until golden on both sides. Slice pork into thin shreds.

Combine sprouts, scallions and cilantro in a bowl. Add dressing and toss to coat. Place a bread slice on each plate and top with salad, shredded pork and caramelized onions. Serve immediately.

Serves 4

Hint

Use rustic or country-style bread if wood-fired bread is unavailable.

Beef and lemongrass kabobs

Soak skewers in water to cover for 15 minutes, then drain. In a bowl, combine steak cubes and 3 tablespoons chili oil and toss to coat. Thread cubes onto skewers, separating them with lemongrass pieces.

Preheat a broiler (grill) or warm a frying pan over high heat. Broil (grill) or fry beef until brown, 6–8 minutes.

Fill a saucepan with water and bring to a boil. Add noodles and cook until tender, about 3 minutes. (Some precooked egg noodles need only to be soaked in hot water for 8 minutes; check package for instructions.) Drain noodles and set aside.

In a small bowl, combine peanut oil, remaining 3 tablespoons chili oil, chili pepper, cilantro, ginger, soy sauce, lime juice, sesame seeds and salt and pepper to taste. Add to cooked noodles and toss to coat evenly.

Serve kabobs with noodles.

Serves 4

12 bamboo skewers

19 oz (590 g) rump steak, cut into
   1-inch (2.5-cm) cubes

6 tablespoons chili oil (see page 52 for recipe)

2 lemongrass stalks, cut into
   1/2-inch (12-mm) pieces

8 oz (250 g) Chinese egg noodles

1/4 cup (2 fl oz / 60 ml) peanut oil

1 small red chili pepper, seeded and chopped

1/2 cup (3/4 oz / 20 g) fresh cilantro
   (fresh coriander) leaves, roughly torn

1 tablespoon peeled and grated fresh ginger

2 tablespoons soy sauce

juice of 2 limes

3 teaspoons sesame seeds, toasted

salt and freshly ground black pepper

lime wedges, for garnish

Chili beef burgers with Asian salad

1 lb (500 g) ground (minced) lean beef

1 clove garlic, crushed

1 small red chili pepper,
   seeded and finely chopped

1 small yellow (brown) onion, grated

2 tablespoons chopped fresh cilantro
   (fresh coriander)

1 tablespoon vegetable oil, for brushing

4 cups (4 oz / 125 g) arugula (rocket)

20 Vietnamese mint leaves

1/2 cup (3/4 oz / 20 g) loosely packed fresh
   cilantro (fresh coriander) leaves

1 tablespoon chili oil (see page 52 for recipe)

salt and freshly ground black pepper

4 crusty rolls, halved

1/4 cup (2 fl oz / 60 ml) Thai sweet chili sauce,
   optional

In a bowl, combine beef, garlic, chili pepper, onion and cilantro. Using wet hands, mix well. Divide into 4 portions and shape each portion into a patty, flattening it slightly to fit size of roll.

Place a frying pan over high heat. Brush both sides of beef patties with vegetable oil and fry until cooked through to center, 3–4 minutes per side.

In a bowl, combine arugula, mint and cilantro. Drizzle with chili oil and season with salt and pepper. Place greens on bottom halves of rolls. Add beef patties and drizzle with Thai sweet chili sauce if desired. Add tops of rolls and serve.

Serves 4

Hint

Bird's eye and serrano chilies are recommended for this recipe.

42

Pork with ginger and lime sauce

In a shallow glass or ceramic dish, combine lime juice, ginger, garlic, honey, soy sauce, sherry and salt and pepper to taste. Add pork and turn to coat with marinade. Cover and refrigerate for 30 minutes.

Bring a saucepan of water to a boil. Add squash and cook until soft, 8–10 minutes. Drain, place in a bowl and mash with a fork or potato masher. Add cilantro and stir to combine. Season with salt and pepper.

Preheat oven to 225°F (110°C / Gas ¼).

Remove pork chops from marinade, reserving marinade. Pat pork dry with paper towels. Warm vegetable oil in a frying pan over medium heat. Add pork and cook until tender, 3–4 minutes per side. Remove from pan, place on a heatproof plate and keep warm in preheated oven. Add reserved marinade to pan, bring to a boil and cook for 1 minute. Divide squash among individual plates. Top with pork, drizzle with warm pan juices and serve.

Serves 4

3 tablespoons fresh lime juice

2 teaspoons peeled and grated fresh ginger

2 cloves garlic, finely chopped

2 tablespoons honey

2 tablespoons soy sauce

3 tablespoons dry sherry

salt and freshly ground black pepper

4 butterfly pork chops, about 3½ oz (105 g) each

1 lb (500 g) butternut squash (pumpkin), peeled, seeded, and cut into 2-inch (5-cm) pieces

¼ cup (¼ oz / 7 g) chopped fresh cilantro (fresh coriander) leaves

3 tablespoons vegetable oil

Warm chickpea salad with chili and lime dressing

2 tablespoons peanut oil

1 yellow (brown) onion, finely chopped

2 cloves garlic, finely chopped

1⅓ cups (14 oz / 440 g) drained,
   canned chickpeas

juice of 2 limes

¼ cup (2 fl oz / 60 ml) chili oil
   (see page 52 for recipe)

½ cup (¾ oz / 20 g) fresh cilantro
   (fresh coriander) leaves

salt and freshly ground black pepper

crusty bread, warmed, for serving

Heat oil in a large frying pan or wok over medium heat. Add onion and garlic and cook until soft, 3–5 minutes. Add chickpeas and stir until heated through, about 3 minutes. Reduce heat to low, add lime juice and cook, stirring, for 1 minute. Add chili oil and cilantro and season with salt and pepper. Serve warm with bread.

Serves 4

Roasted vegetables with Thai herbs

Preheat oven to 400°F (200°C / Gas 6). Place bell peppers, onions, beets, potatoes, squash, sweet potato, zucchini, garlic, lemongrass and 4 lime leaves in a large roasting pan. Drizzle with chili oil and toss until all vegetables are coated. Sprinkle liberally with salt and pepper. Bake until vegetables are tender, turning 2 or 3 times, 30–40 minutes.

Remove from oven and discard lime leaves and lemongrass. Arrange vegetables on individual plates. Drizzle with lime juice and garnish with chopped cilantro and lime leaves. Accompany with bread and olive oil.

Serves 4–6

1 red bell pepper (capsicum),
   seeded and quartered
1 yellow bell pepper (capsicum),
   seeded and quartered
3 red (Spanish) onions, peeled and quartered
10 oz (300 g) beets (beetroots),
   trimmed and quartered
1 lb (500 g) potatoes, quartered
1 lb (500 g) butternut squash (pumpkin),
   peeled and cubed
20 oz (625 g) sweet potato (kumara),
   peeled and cubed
10 oz (300 g) zucchini (courgette),
   cut into 2-inch (5-cm) slices
8 whole cloves garlic, unpeeled
3 lemongrass stalks,
   cut into 2-inch (5-cm) lengths
4 kaffir lime leaves
   or 1 tablespoon grated lime zest
1/2 cup (4 fl oz / 120 ml) chili oil
   (see page 52 for recipe)
sea salt and freshly ground black pepper
1 cup (8 fl oz / 125 ml) fresh lime juice
2 tablespoons chopped fresh cilantro (fresh
   coriander) leaves, for garnish
4 kaffir lime leaves
   or 1 teaspoon grated lime zest, for garnish
crusty bread, for serving
good-quality virgin olive oil, for serving

Hint

To ensure that the vegetables roast evenly, cut them into similar-sized pieces.

Smoked rainbow trout and chili salad

⅓ cup (1½ oz / 45 g) unsweetened dried
   (desiccated) shredded coconut

¾ cup (6 fl oz / 180 ml) water

1½ teaspoons sambal oelek
   (see page 52 for recipe)

4 scallions (shallots / spring onions), sliced

1 clove garlic, chopped

⅓ cup (3 fl oz / 90 ml) fresh lime juice

10 oz (300 g) smoked rainbow trout,
   roughly chopped

2 cups (2 oz / 60 g) bean sprouts

1 cup (1 oz / 30 g) baby arugula (rocket)
   leaves, chopped

Combine coconut, water, sambal oelek, scallions and garlic in a small saucepan over medium heat. Bring to a boil, stirring, and cook for 2 minutes. Remove from heat and allow to cool completely. Stir in lime juice. Chill until ready to serve.

In a bowl, combine trout, bean sprouts and arugula. Fold in coconut mixture. Serve chilled.

Serves 2 or 3

Asian coconut and crisp vegetable salad

Combine water, coconut, shrimp paste, chili powder, garlic and sugar in a small saucepan. Place over medium heat, stir until mixture boils and cook for 3 minutes. Remove from heat and allow to cool completely. Stir in lime juice. Chill coconut mixture until ready to serve.

In a large bowl, combine watercress, carrot, radishes, cucumber, bean sprouts, scallions and lime leaves. Toss until well combined. Add coconut mixture and toss again. Serve immediately.

Serves 4

1 cup (8 fl oz / 250 ml) water
1/2 cup (2 oz / 60 g) unsweetened dried (desiccated) shredded coconut
1 teaspoon shrimp paste
1 teaspoon chili powder or to taste
1 clove garlic, finely chopped
1/2 teaspoon brown sugar
2 tablespoons fresh lime juice
2 cups (2 1/2 oz / 75 g) watercress
1 carrot, peeled and julienned
8 small red radishes, trimmed and julienned
1/2 English (hothouse) cucumber, peeled, seeded and thinly sliced
1 cup (4 oz / 125 g) bean sprouts
4 scallions (shallots / spring onions), sliced
2 kaffir lime leaves, finely shredded or 1/2 teaspoon grated lime zest

Tofu with vegetables, chili and sesame

2 tablespoons oyster sauce

1 tablespoon water

2 teaspoons soy sauce

2 tablespoons vegetable oil

2 cloves garlic, finely chopped

2 teaspoons peeled and grated fresh ginger

2 small red chili peppers,
  seeded and thinly sliced

1 red bell pepper (capsicum), seeded and sliced

1 bunch choy sum, about 16 oz (500 g), trimmed
  and cut into in 2½-inch (6-cm) lengths

8 long beans, trimmed and cut
  into 2 ½-inch (6-cm) lengths

5 oz (150 g) fried tofu puffs,
  cut into 1-inch (2.5-cm) cubes

3 teaspoons sesame seeds, toasted, for garnish

I n a small bowl, combine oyster sauce, water and soy sauce. In a wok over medium heat, warm vegetable oil. Add garlic, ginger and chili peppers and stir-fry until aromatic, 1–2 minutes. Add bell pepper, choy sum and beans and stir-fry until slightly softened, 2–3 minutes. Add tofu and oyster sauce mixture. Toss until tofu and vegetables are well coated and tofu is heated through, 3–4 minutes. Serve hot, garnished with sesame seeds.

Serves 4

Hints

If tofu puffs are unavailable, fry your own tofu pieces. To fry tofu pieces: Cut 6½ oz (200 g) firm tofu into 1-inch (2.5-cm) cubes. In a wok, over medium heat, warm ¼ cup (2 fl oz / 60 ml) vegetable oil. Working in batches, add tofu and stir-fry until golden on all sides, 2–3 minutes. Using a slotted spoon, remove from wok and drain on paper towels.
Bird's eye and serrano chilies are recommended for this recipe.

Crab and lime salad on betel leaves

To make dressing: Place lime juice, vinegar, sesame and olive oils and fish sauce in a screw-top jar. Shake to combine and set aside. In a bowl, combine crabmeat, chili pepper, scallions, cilantro, lime leaves, coconut, cucumber and mint. Add dressing and gently mix until well combined. Place 2 betel leaves on each plate. Spoon salad onto leaves. Serve with lime wedges.

Serves 6

FOR DRESSING

3 tablespoons fresh lime juice

2 tablespoons coconut vinegar
   (available from Asian markets)

1 teaspoon Asian sesame oil

1 tablespoon olive oil

2 teaspoons fish sauce

1 lb (500 g) fresh or canned crabmeat,
   well drained

1 small red chili pepper,
   seeded and thinly sliced

6 scallions (shallots / spring onions), sliced

2 tablespoons chopped fresh cilantro
   (fresh coriander)

3 kaffir lime leaves, finely shredded
   or 1 teaspoon grated lime zest

$\frac{1}{4}$ cup ($1\frac{1}{2}$ oz / 45 g) shaved fresh coconut,
   cut into fine strips

$\frac{1}{4}$ small English (hothouse) cucumber,
   seeded and thinly sliced

2 tablespoons chopped fresh Vietnamese mint

12 fresh betel leaves

6 lime wedges, for serving

Hint

Use white vinegar if coconut vinegar is unavailable.

Stir-fried choy sum with ginger

3 tablespoons fish sauce

3 tablespoons water

2 teaspoons peeled and grated fresh ginger

2 tablespoons vegetable oil

1 bunch choy sum, about 16 oz (500 g),
    trimmed and cut into 3-inch (7.5-cm) lengths

In a small bowl, combine fish sauce, water and ginger. Warm vegetable oil in a wok over medium heat. Add choy sum and stir-fry until slightly softened and color intensifies, about 3 minutes. Stir in fish sauce mixture and toss until choy sum is well coated. Cover and cook for 2 minutes. Serve hot.

Serves 4

condiments.

Tomato salsa with chili and cilantro

In a bowl, combine tomatoes, chili pepper, onion and cilantro. Combine balsamic vinegar and lime juice in a small bowl, mix well and add to tomato mixture. Stir and season with salt and pepper. Cover and allow to stand at room temperature for 15 minutes before serving.

Serves 4–6

2 large vine-ripened tomatoes, chopped
1 small red chili pepper, seeded and chopped
1/2 small red (Spanish) onion, chopped
1/3 cup (1/2 oz / 10 g) chopped fresh cilantro (fresh coriander)
2 tablespoons balsamic vinegar
1 tablespoon fresh lime juice
sea salt and freshly ground black pepper

Hint

The salsa is excellent with hot-and-spicy money bags, duck on a bed of chili onions, spicy oven-roasted chicken, chili-noodle cakes and lime shrimp with spicy Thai pesto. It also makes a delicious accompaniment for fried wontons and grilled fish or chicken.

Bird's eye or serrano chilies are recommended for this recipe.

Sambal oelek

1 lb (500 g) red chili peppers
2¹/₂ cups water (20 fl oz / 625 ml)
1 tablespoon white vinegar
1 teaspoon superfine (caster) sugar
2 tablespoons peanut oil
¹/₂ cup (4 fl oz / 125 ml) boiling water

This mixture of red chili peppers, vinegar and salt is used throughout Asian cooking as a flavoring and as a spicy hot condiment. Remove stems from chili peppers. Remove seeds if you want less fiery sambal oelek. Place chilies and water in a saucepan over medium heat and bring to a boil. Cover, reduce heat to simmer and cook until chilies are soft, about 15 minutes. Drain. Working in batches, place chili peppers in a food processor and process until smooth. Add vinegar, sugar, peanut oil and boiling water and process to combine. Pour into sterilized jars, seal and refrigerate for up to 1 month.

Makes about 1¹/₂ cups (12 fl oz / 375 ml)

Hint

Sambal oelek can be frozen in ice cube trays to make easy-to-use portions. Bird's eye or serrano chilies are recommended for this recipe.

Chili oil

about 10 oz (300 g) red chili peppers
1 cup (8 fl oz / 250 ml) olive oil

This is a good way of preserving chili peppers if you have an abundance. The oil is milder than commercial chili oil and is not red in color. Use for stir-fries, dressings and marinades and as a condiment when serving Asian foods.
Wash and dry chili peppers. Trim any long stems with kitchen scissors. Pack chilies into a sterilized jar. Add enough oil to completely cover chilies. Seal jars and store in a cool, dark place. Replenish oil after use and always be sure that chilies are covered with oil and jar is tightly sealed. Chili oil will keep for up to 3 months.

Makes 1 jar (16 fl oz / 500 ml)

Mango, papaya and green chili relish

In a small bowl, combine mango, papaya, chili pepper, scallions and lime leaf. Stir in lime juice and sesame oil. Mix well. Cover and chill for 30 minutes.

Serves 4

1 small ripe mango, peeled, pitted and chopped
¼ small papaya, peeled, seeded and chopped
½ long green chili pepper,
   seeded and finely chopped
6 scallions (shallots / spring onions), sliced
1 kaffir lime leaf, finely shredded or
   ½ teaspoon grated lime zest
3 tablespoons fresh lime juice
2 teaspoons Asian sesame oil

Hint

Serve the relish with hot-and-spicy money bags, spicy oven-roasted chicken, chili-noodle cakes, duck on a bed of chili onions, or as an accompaniment to grilled chicken or fish.

Red curry paste

6 cloves garlic, roughly chopped

6 small red chili peppers, roughly chopped

3 tablespoons chopped lemongrass

1 tablespoon grated fresh galangal
   or 2 teaspoons galangal powder

1/2 yellow (brown) onion, roughly chopped

2 tablespoons roughly chopped fresh cilantro
   (fresh coriander)

1/3 cup (3 fl oz / 90 ml) vegetable oil

1 teaspoon ground coriander

1 teaspoon ground cumin

1 tablespoon ground paprika

1 teaspoon shrimp paste

Place all ingredients in a food processor. Process until a thick paste forms. Transfer to a sterilized screw-top jar. Seal and store in refrigerator for up to 1 month.

Makes about 2/3 cup (5 fl oz / 150 ml)

Green curry paste

4 cloves garlic, roughly chopped

3 tablespoons chopped lemongrass

2 teaspoons grated fresh galangal
   or 1 teaspoon galangal powder

4 long green chili peppers

6 scallions (shallots / spring onions),
   roughly chopped

1/2 cup (3/4 oz / 25 g) roughly chopped fresh
   cilantro (fresh coriander)

1/3 cup (3 fl oz / 90 ml) vegetable oil

1/2 teaspoon ground coriander

1/2 teaspoon ground cumin

2 teaspoons grated lime zest (rind)

1 tablespoon shrimp paste

Place all ingredients in a food processor and process until a thick paste forms. Transfer to a sterilized screw-top jar. Seal and store in refrigerator for up to 1 month.

Makes about 3/4 cup (6 fl oz / 180 ml)

desserts

Pistachio and cardamom ice cream

Combine sugar, cardamom pods, evaporated milk and cream in a heavy-bottomed saucepan. Place over medium heat and stir for 10 minutes; do not allow to boil. Remove from heat and stir in pistachio nuts. Allow mixture to cool to room temperature. Pour mixture into four 1-cup (8-fl oz / 250 ml) molds and freeze overnight. Remove ice cream from molds and serve with slices of fresh mango if desired.

This Indian ice cream is refreshing after a hot, spicy meal.

Serves 4

½ cup (3½ oz / 105 g) superfine (caster) sugar
5 cardamom pods, bruised
3 cups (24 fl oz / 750 ml) evaporated milk
¾ cup (6 fl oz / 180 ml) thickened cream
  or heavy (double) cream
1 cup (4 oz / 125 g) shelled pistachio nuts,
  finely chopped
slices of fresh mango, optional, for serving

Hint

Disposable paper cups make good molds for the ice cream. After the ice cream freezes, the cups can easily be peeled away.

Ginger and nutmeg sweet potato pudding

10 oz (300 g) sweet potato (kumara),
  peeled and roughly chopped
1 cup (8 fl oz / 250 ml) thick coconut cream
$\frac{1}{4}$ cup (2 oz / 60 g) brown sugar
2 eggs, beaten
2 teaspoons peeled and grated fresh ginger
2 teaspoons freshly grated nutmeg
  or 2 teaspoons ground nutmeg
whipped cream, optional, for garnish

Preheat oven to 350°F (180°C / Gas 4). Line a bamboo steamer with parchment (baking) paper or use a heatproof plate. Half fill a wok with water (steamer should not touch water) and bring water to a boil. Arrange sweet potato in steamer, cover and place steamer in wok. Cook sweet potato until tender, adding more water to wok when necessary, about 15 minutes. Lift steamer from wok, carefully remove sweet potato from steamer and transfer to a bowl. Mash with a fork or potato masher until smooth. Set aside and allow to cool.

Place sweet potato, coconut cream, brown sugar, eggs, ginger and nutmeg in a food processor and process until smooth. Pour into 6 Chinese teacups or other heatproof molds. Place on a baking sheet (tray) and cook until firm to the touch, about 20 minutes. Remove from oven. Serve warm or chilled, garnished with whipped cream if desired.

Makes 6

Mango and cumin lassi

³/₄ teaspoon cumin seeds
1¹/₄ cups (10 oz / 300 g) plain yogurt
1¹/₄ cups (10 fl oz / 300 ml) nonfat milk
1 ripe mango, peeled, pitted and chopped
superfine (caster) sugar to taste
crushed ice, for serving

Place cumin seeds in a nonstick pan over medium heat and toast until aromatic, 1–2 minutes. Remove from pan and allow to cool. Place ½ teaspoon cumin seeds, yogurt, milk and mango in a food processor and process until thick. Sweeten to taste with sugar. Place a handful of crushed ice into each glass. Pour lassi over ice. Serve immediately, sprinkled lightly with remaining cumin seeds.

This cool, refreshing drink is ideal for serving with or after a spicy meal.

Serves 4

Chilled spice tea

2 long red chili peppers, halved
2 lemongrass stalks, sliced
1 piece fresh ginger, about 2 inches
   (5 cm) long, peeled and sliced
¹/₄ cup (2 oz / 60 g) brown sugar
4 cups (32 fl oz / 1 L) boiling water
6–8 sprigs fresh Vietnamese mint
crushed ice, optional

Place chili peppers, lemongrass, ginger and brown sugar in a heatproof pitcher. Add boiling water and steep for 5 minutes. Strain into a porcelain or glass teapot. Refrigerate for 1 hour or more.

To serve, place mint sprigs into small serving glasses and add chilled tea. Add crushed ice if desired.

Serves 6–8

glossary

Asian sesame oil: Rich, dark- or golden-colored oil extracted from sesame seeds. Oil made from toasted seeds has a pronounced nutty flavor.

banana leaves: Large leaves from the banana plant, used to line bamboo steamers or for wrapping foods prior to steaming. Parchment (baking) paper may be substituted. The leaves are available fresh or frozen.

bean sprouts: Sprouted beans and peas add a fresh flavor and crunchy texture to salads and other Asian dishes. Mung bean sprouts are sold fresh or canned. Snow pea (mange-tout) sprouts are available fresh. Fresh sprouts are preferred for their clean taste and crisp texture; store in refrigerator for up to 3 days.

bok choy: Asian variety of cabbage with dark green leaves and thick white stems. Sizes vary from baby bok choy about 6 inches (15 cm) long to bok choy as long as a celery stalk.

chili oil. Spicy oil produced by steeping red chili peppers in oil. It is available bottled or you can prepare your own (see page 52 for recipe).

Chinese dried mushrooms: Intensely flavorful, dark mushrooms that need to be rehydrated before use. The stems are discarded. Flavorful fresh mushrooms make an acceptable substitute.

Chinese roast duck: Sold freshly roasted in Chinese markets, these ducks are seasoned and glazed before roasting to yield moist, flavorful meat. Use 1–2 days after purchase. Roast chicken may be substituted.

choy sum: Also known as flowering cabbage, this mild-flavored Chinese green has thin stalks bearing leaves and yellow flowers, all of which are used in cooking.

coconut milk and cream: Grated coconut flesh steeped in water yields a rich liquid called coconut milk. The particularly thick substance that rises to the top of coconut milk is coconut cream and can be removed for use in Thai desserts and other recipes.

coconut vinegar: Sweet tasting, cloudy white vinegar made from coconuts and sold in bottles in Asian markets.

curry paste: Condiment consisting of curry seasonings and red or green chili peppers. Both red and green curry pastes are available bottled, or you may make your own versions (see page 54 for recipe).

egg noodles: Used extensively in Asian cooking, these noodles are available fresh or dried in a variety of widths: thin, round or flat.

fish sauce: Pungent sauce of salted, fermented fish and other seasonings, used in cooking and as a dipping sauce. Products vary in intensity based on the country of origin. Fish sauce from Thailand, called nam pla, is a commonly available variety.

long bean: Related to the black-eyed pea, this thin, flexible but crisp-textured green bean is cut into short lengths before cooking. Long beans are also called snake beans and yard-long beans, though most found in markets are 24 inches (60 cm) or less in length.

oyster sauce: Thick, dark brown Chinese sauce made from fermented dried oysters and soy sauce, and sold in bottles. It is used to add a mild or intense briny flavor to stir-fries and other dishes.

rice: A wide variety of rice is used in Asian cooking. Glutinous rice types, sometimes called sticky rices for their consistency, have a high percentage of gluten. These short- or long-grain varieties are often used in desserts. Nonglutinous rice types, with their lower gluten content, cook to form separate, fluffy grains and are used to accompany curries and other Asian dishes. Jasmine rice is a nonglutinous, long-grain Thai variety known for its appealing fragrance and taste.

rice wine: Sweet, low-alcohol Chinese wine, also known as shaoxing wine, made from fermented glutinous rice. Sake or dry sherry can be substituted.

sambal oelek: Indonesian paste consisting of ground chili peppers combined with salt and occasionally vinegar. This spicy condiment is available bottled, or you can prepare your own (see page 52 for recipe).

shiitake mushroom: Meaty mushroom with light or dark brown caps. Shiitakes are available fresh or dried.

shrimp paste: Produced by drying, salting and pounding shrimp into a pungent-flavored paste that is then formed into blocks or cakes.

tamarind pulp: The ripe fruit of the large tropical tamarind tree is dried and seasoned, and the resulting tart pulp is packaged in jars sold in Asian markets. If unavailable, substitute fresh lime juice.

Thai sweet chili sauce: Mild chili sauce with a sweet aftertaste, used to flavor dishes during cooking and often as a dipping sauce.

udon noodles. Soft, pale Japanese noodles made from wheat and available fresh or dried and in several widths.

water chestnut: Tuber of a plant grown in Asia, round in shape with subtle sweet, crunchy, light-colored flesh. Water chestnuts are widely available canned. After opening, store in clean water in the refrigerator for up to 3 weeks.

wonton wrapper: Thin sheets of wheat- or egg-based dough, circular or square in shape, used to enclose a variety of fillings. They are available fresh or frozen.

index

Parsley, Chinese (cilantro) 14
Pesto, spicy Thai 32
Pistachio and cardamom ice cream 55
Poached chicken in green coconut sauce 37
Pork
    with ginger and lime sauce 43
    shredded, on spicy bruschetta 40
Potato
    and bok choy soup 22
    and leek vichyssoise with Thai herbs 21
    soup, rustic, with Thai spices 19
Prawns see Shrimp
Pudding, ginger and nutmeg sweet potato 56

Rainbow trout, smoked with chili salad 46
Red curry
    noodles with green vegetables 27
    paste 54
    shrimp 34
Relish, mango, papaya and green chili 53
Rice
    parcels, saffron 25
    star anise and roast duck risotto 24
Risotto, star anise and roast duck 24
Roast duck and star anise risotto 24
Roasted vegetables with Thai herbs 45
Rustic potato soup with Thai spices 19

Saffron rice parcels 25
Salad
    Asian coconut and vegetable 47
    crab and lime, on betel leaves 49
    smoked rainbow trout and chili 46
    tofu with vegetables, chili and sesame 48
    warm chickpea, with chili and lime dressing 44
Salsa, tomato, with chili and cilantro 51
Sambal oelek 52
Sauce
    chili 53
    mango, papaya and green chili relish 53
    sambal oelek 54
Spicy Thai pesto 32
    tomato salsa with chili and cilantro 51
Seafood dumplings, steamed 29
Shredded pork on spicy bruschetta 40
Shrimp
    and lemongrass sticks 31
    lime, with spicy Thai pesto 32
    red curry 34
Smoked rainbow trout and chili salad 46

Soup
    Asian vegetable and lentil 20
    bok choy and potato 22
    carrot, with Asian greens and coconut 23
    rustic potato, with Thai spices 19
    spicy squash and bean 18
    vichyssoise with Thai herbs 21
Spiced tea, chilled 57
Spicy chicken with basil 35
Spicy oven-roasted chicken 38
Spicy squash and bean soup 18
Spicy Thai pesto 32
Squash and bean soup, spicy 18
Star anise and roast duck risotto 24
Steamed lemon-pepper fish 30
Steamed seafood dumplings 29
Stir-fried choy sum with ginger 50
Sweet potato pudding, ginger and nutmeg 56

Tea, chilled spice 57
Thai basil 15
Thai ginger (galangal) 14
Thai herbs
    with roasted vegetables 45
    with Vichyssoise 21
Thai pesto, spicy 32
Thai spicy chicken with basil 35
Tofu with vegetables, chili and sesame 48
Tomato salsa with chili and cilantro 51
Trout, smoked rainbow, and chili salad 46

Vegetables
    crisp, and coconut salad, Asian 47
    green, with red curry noodles 27
    and lentil soup, Asian 20
    roasted, with Thai herbs 45
    with tofu, chili and sesame 48
Vichyssoise with Thai herbs 21
Vietnamese mint 15

Warm chickpea salad with chili and lime dressing 44
Wraps, fish 28

Guide to weights and measures

The conversions given in the recipes in this book are approximate. Whichever system you use, remember to follow it consistently, thereby ensuring that the proportions are consistent throughout a recipe.

WEIGHTS

Imperial	Metric
1/3 oz	10 g
1/2 oz	15 g
3/4 oz	20 g
1 oz	30 g
2 oz	60 g
3 oz	90 g
4 oz (1/4 lb)	125 g
5 oz (1/3 lb)	150 g
6 oz	180 g
7 oz	220 g
8 oz (1/2 lb)	250 g
9 oz	280 g
10 oz	300 g
11 oz	330 g
12 oz (3/4 lb)	375 g
16 oz (1 lb)	500 g
2 lb	1 kg
3 lb	1.5 kg
4 lb	2 kg

VOLUME

Imperial	Metric	Cup
1 fl oz	30 ml	
2 fl oz	60 ml	1/4
3 fl oz	90 ml	1/3
4 fl oz	125 ml	1/2
5 fl oz	150 ml	2/3
6 fl oz	180 ml	3/4
8 fl oz	250 ml	1
10 fl oz	300 ml	1 1/4
12 fl oz	375 ml	1 1/2
13 fl oz	400 ml	1 2/3
14 fl oz	440 ml	1 3/4
16 fl oz	500 ml	2
24 fl oz	750 ml	3
32 fl oz	1L	4

USEFUL CONVERSIONS

1/4 teaspoon	1.25 ml
1/2 teaspoon	2.5 ml
1 teaspoon	5 ml
1 Australian tablespoon	20 ml (4 teaspoons)
1 UK/US tablespoon	15 ml (3 teaspoons)

Butter/Shortening

1 tablespoon	1/2 oz	15 g
1 1/2 tablespoons	3/4 oz	20 g
2 tablespoons	1 oz	30 g
3 tablespoons	1 1/2 oz	45 g

OVEN TEMPERATURE GUIDE

The Celsius (°C) and Fahrenheit (°F) temperatures in this chart apply to most electric ovens. Decrease by 25°F or 10°C for a gas oven or refer to the manufacturer's temperature guide. For temperatures below 325°F (160°C), do not decrease the given temperature.

Oven description	°C	°F	Gas Mark
Cool	110	225	1/4
	130	250	1/2
Very slow	140	275	1
	150	300	2
Slow	170	325	3
Moderate	180	350	4
	190	375	5
Moderately Hot	200	400	6
Fairly Hot	220	425	7
Hot	230	450	8
Very Hot	240	475	9
Extremely Hot	250	500	10

First published in the United States in 2002 by Periplus Editions (HK) Ltd., with editorial offices at 153 Milk Street, Boston, Massachusetts 02109 and 130 Joo Seng Road #06-01/03 Olivine Building Singapore 368357

Commissioned by Deborah Nixon; Text: Vicki Liley; Photographer: Ben Dearnley; Stylist: Vicki Liley; Design Concepts: Kerry Klinner; Editor: Carolyn Miller; Production Manager: Sally Stokes; Project Co-ordinator: Alexandra Nahlous

© Copyright 2002 Lansdowne Publishing Pty Ltd

Printed in India